WG

Friends Are Forever

Friends Are Forever

A Treasury of Quotations about
Laughter, Loyalty, Sharing and Trust

Compiled and Edited by Criswell Freeman

WALNUT GROVE PRESS
Nashville, TN 37205

ISBN 1-887655-78-6

The ideas expressed in this book are not, in all cases, exact quotations, as some have been edited for clarity and brevity. In all cases, the author has attempted to maintain the speaker's original intent. In some cases, material for this book was obtained from secondary sources, primarily print media. While every effort was made to ensure the accuracy of these sources, the accuracy cannot be guaranteed. For additions, deletions, corrections or clarifications in future editions of this text, please write WALNUT GROVE PRESS.

Printed in the United States of America
Typesetting & Page Layout by Sue Gerdes
Editor for Walnut Grove Press: Alan Ross
2 3 4 5 6 7 8 9 10 •   99 00 01 02

ACKNOWLEDGMENTS
The author gratefully acknowledges the helpful support of Angela Freeman, Dick and Mary Freeman, Mary Susan Freeman, and Jim Gallery.

For Angela,
My Best Friend

Table of Contents

Introduction

Emily Dickinson spoke for friends everywhere when she observed, "My friends are my estate." Dickinson understood that friends are among our most treasured possessions. But unlike a bank account or a stock certificate, the value of a true friendship is beyond measure.

This book celebrates the joys of building and preserving *your* personal estate of lifelong friends. On these pages, you will enjoy friendly advice from a collection of experts. You'll read quotations about laughter, loyalty, sharing, and trust. You'll be reminded of what it means to aid an ally, to back a backer, or to console a comrade. You may even be inspired to pick up the telephone and reconnect with a long-lost pal. If so, you will have increased two personal fortunes at once. And take it from Emily Dickinson: That's smart estate planning.

1

A Friend Is...

What is a friend? A thesaurus offers many synonyms: companion, partner, helper, co-worker, colleague, ally, chum, pal, and alter ego, to name but a few. Like the people who create them, each friendship is unique. But one thing is certain: Enduring friendship, while difficult to cubbyhole, is easy to recognize. We know it when we see it.

Epicurus wrote, "Of all the things that wisdom provides to make life happy, by far the greatest is friendship." Over two thousand years have passed since the Greek sage offered this observation, but little has changed. Friendships are still among the most sublime of human pleasures.

The following quotations describe, at least in part, what it means to be a friend. If you're interested in acquiring one of life's greatest possessions, turn the page.

F riendship is a single soul
dwelling in two bodies.

Aristotle

A friend may well be reckoned
the masterpiece of nature.

Ralph Waldo Emerson

A friend is like a poem.

Persian Proverb

F riends are relatives you make for yourself.

Eustache Deschamps

A friend is a present
you give yourself.

Robert Louis Stevenson

Friendship may be defined as an accord
joined with mutual goodwill and affection.

Cicero

Friendship is a strong and habitual inclination
in two persons to promote the good
and happiness of one another.

Eustace Budgell

My best friend is the man who in wishing me
well wishes it for my sake.

Aristotle

Friendship is a word the very sight of which
in print makes the heart warm.

Augustine Birrell

The real friend is another self.

Cicero

True friendship is self-love at secondhand.

William Hazlitt

A Friend Is...

True friends ... face in the same direction
toward common projects, interests and goals.

C. S. Lewis

A real friend feels no need to excuse himself
for some failing.

The Lubliner Rabbi

A friend is one who makes me do my best.

Oswald Chambers

Friends are an aid to the young, to guard
them from error; to the elderly, to attend
to their wants; to those in the prime of life,
to assist them to noble deeds.

Aristotle

Without friends no one would choose
to live, though he had all other goods.

Aristotle

One who knows how to show and
to accept kindness will be a friend
better than any possession.

Sophocles

My friend is he who will tell me my faults,
in private.

Ibn Gabirol

A faithful friend is the medicine of life.

Old Proverb

Each friend represents a world in us, a world possibly not born until they arrive, and it is only by this meeting that a new world is born.

Anaïs Nin

True friends are the ones who really know you but love you anyway.

Edna Buchanan

Friendship's a noble name. 'Tis love refined.

Susannah Centlivre

The balm of life — a kind and faithful friend.

Mercy Otis Warren

A friend can tell you things you don't want
to tell yourself.

Frances Ward Weller

She is a friend. She gathers the pieces and
gives them back to me in all the right order.

Toni Morrison

Acquaintances ask about our outward life;
friends ask about our inner life.

Marie von Ebner-Eschenbach

Best friend, my wellspring in the wilderness!

George Eliot

Friendship is the bread of the heart.

Mary Russell Mitford

2

The Art of Friendship

The philosopher William James observed, "Human beings are born into this little span of life, and among the best things that life has to offer are its friendships and intimacies. Yet, humans leave their friendships with no cultivation, letting them grow as they will by the roadside." James understood that when we leave our friendships unattended, the resulting harvest is predictably slim.

Ralph Waldo Emerson advised, "The only way to have a friend is to be one." Emerson realized that a lasting relationship, like a bountiful garden, must be tended with care. In this chapter, we consider the art of cultivating friends. If you take these words to heart, your harvest will last a lifetime.

Friendship is an art, and
very few persons are born
with a natural gift for it.

Kathleen Norris

To have a good friend is one of the highest delights of life; to be a good friend is one of the noblest and most difficult undertakings.

Unknown

I am quite sure that no friendship yields its true pleasure and nobility of nature without frequent communication, sympathy and service.

George E. Woodberry

Those who cannot give friendship will rarely receive it and never hold it.

Dagobert D. Runes

Hold a true friend with both hands.

African Proverb

Friends are lost by calling often and calling seldom.

Scottish Proverb

Friendship with oneself is all-important,
because without it one cannot be friends
with anyone else in the world.

Eleanor Roosevelt

Be a friend to thyself, and others
will be so too.

Thomas Fuller

Confidence is the foundation of friendship.
If we give it, we will receive it.

Harry E. Humphreys, Jr.

Radiate friendship
and it will return sevenfold.

B. C. Forbes

Friendship requires great communication.

Saint Francis de Sales

Give and take makes good friends.

Scottish Proverb

Friendship takes time.

Agnes Repplier

Friendship is a plant
        which must be often watered.

Unknown

Go oft to the house of thy friend,
        for weeds choke the unused path.

Ralph Waldo Emerson

'T is the privilege of friendship to talk
nonsense and have nonsense respected.

Charles Lamb

If you want to be listened to, you should put
in time listening.

Marge Piercy

To make people into friends, listen to them
for hours at a time.

Rebecca West

You can make more friends in two months
by becoming interested in other people
than you can in two years by trying
to get other people interested in you.

Dale Carnegie

Friendship is the pleasing game
　　　　of interchanging praise.
Oliver Wendell Holmes, Sr.

Many a friendship — long, loyal, and
　　self-sacrificing — rested at first upon no
　　thicker a foundation than a kind word.
Frederick W. Faber

Politeness is an inexpensive way
　　　　of making friends.
William Feather

Of all the things you wear, your expression
　　　　is the most important.
Janet Lane

If we all told what we know of one another,
there would not be four friends in the world.
Blaise Pascal

When anger rises, think of the consequences.
Confucius

Keep the other person's well-being in mind
when you feel an attack of soul-purging truth
coming on.
Betty White

The best rule of friendship is to keep
your heart a little softer than your head.
Unknown

To find a friend one must close one eye.
To keep him — two.

Norman Douglas

When my friends lack an eye,
I look at them in profile.

Joseph Joubert

Who seeks a faultless friend
remains friendless.

Turkish Proverb

The art of being wise is knowing
what to overlook.

William James

To be social is to be forgiving.

Robert Frost

Two persons cannot long be friends if they cannot forgive each other's little failings.

Jean de La Bruyère

Friendship flourishes at the fountain of forgiveness.

William Arthur Ward

What I cannot love, I overlook. That is friendship.

Anaïs Nin

Scatter seeds of kindness.

George Ade

One who knows how to show and to accept kindness will be a friend better than any possession.

Sophocles

Actions, not words, are the true criteria of the attachment of friends.

George Washington

It is not the services we render them,
but the services they render us,
that attach people to us.

Labiche et Morton

When befriended, remember it.
When you befriend, forget it.

Poor Richard's Almanac

Don't ask of your friends
what you yourself can do.

Quintus Ennius

Cooperation is spelled with two letters: WE.

George M. Verity

Friendship without self-interest is rare
and beautiful.

James Francis Byrnes

He who looks for advantage out
of friendship strips it all of its nobility.

Seneca

Live for thy neighbor if thou wouldst live
for thyself.

Seneca

We all remain better friends —
at a slight distance.

Old Saying

A friend to everybody and nobody
is the same thing.

Spanish Proverb

Friendship, by its very nature, is freer of deceit than any other relationship.

Francine du Plessix Gray

Loyalty is what we seek in friendship.

Cicero

Friendships, like marriages, are dependent on avoiding the unforgivable.

John D. MacDonald

You can keep your friends by not giving them away.

Mary Pettibone Poole

The goodness, beauty and perfection of a human being belongs to the one who knows how to recognize these qualities.

Georgette Leblanc

We awaken in others the same attitude
of mind we hold toward them.

Elbert Hubbard

We should behave to our friends as we
would wish our friends to behave to us.

Aristotle

Happiness is achieved only by making
others happy.

Stuart Cloete

Friendship is in loving
rather than being loved.

Robert Seymour Bridges

All the law is fulfilled in one word, even in this; Thou shalt love thy neighbor as thyself.

Galatians 5:14

Silences make the real conversations
between friends.

Margaret Lee Runbeck

True friendship comes when silence
between two people is comfortable.

Dave Tyson Gentry

There is nothing we like to see so much as
the gleam of pleasure in a person's eye when
he feels that we have understood him.

Don Marquis

There can be no friendship when there is
no freedom. Friendship loves the free air
and will not be fenced up in straight
and narrow enclosures.

William Penn

Other people are like a mirror which reflects
back on us the kind of image we cast.

Bishop Fulton J. Sheen

Lead the life that will make you kindly and
friendly to everyone about you, and you will
be surprised what a happy life you will live.

Charles M. Schwab

The most beautiful discovery true friends make is that they can grow separately without growing apart.

Elizabeth Foley

<u>3</u>

Trust

Cicero wrote, "Loyalty is what we seek in a friendship." He was right. Without loyalty, true friendship is impossible. But with loyalty, true friendship is inevitable. Through the quotations that follow, we examine the foundation of any friendship worthy of the name. That foundation is trust.

No soul is desolate as long as there is
a human being for whom it can feel trust
and reverence.

George Eliot

Few delights can equal the mere presence
of one whom we trust utterly.

George Macdonald

A man who doesn't trust himself
can never really trust anyone else.

Cardinal de Retz

They are most deceived that trusteth only
in themselves.

Elizabeth I of England

Surely we ought to prize those friends
on whose principles and opinions we may
constantly rely.

Hannah Farnham Lee

Trust men and they will trust you;
treat them greatly and they will show
themselves great.

Ralph Waldo Emerson

The only way to make a man trustworthy
is to trust him.

Henry Stimson

Trust begets truth.

Sir William Gurney Benham

Confidence is the only bond of friendship.

Publilius Syrus

Nothing wounds a friend like a want
of confidence.

Jean Baptiste Lacordaire

A friend is a person with whom I may
be sincere. Before him, I may think aloud.

Ralph Waldo Emerson

I always felt that the great high privilege, relief, and comfort of friendship was that one had to explain nothing.

Katherine Mansfield

Without trust, the mind's lot is a hard one.

Bettina von Arnim

There's a kind of emotional exploration you plumb with a friend that you don't really do with your family.

Bette Midler

It is a vice to trust all and equally a vice
to trust none.

Seneca

Love all, trust a few.

William Shakespeare

Better trust all and be deceived than doubt
one heart that, if believed, had blessed one's
life with true believing.

Fanny Kemble

The man who trusts other men will make
fewer mistakes than he who distrusts them.

Camillo Benso

If it wasn't for trusting, there would be no living in this world; we couldn't even eat hash with any safety.

Josh Billings

Let us move on and step out boldly, though it be into the night, and we can scarcely see the way. A Higher Intelligence than the mortal sees the road before us.

Charles B. Newcomb

A man who trusts nobody is apt to be the kind of man nobody trusts.

Harold Macmillan

It is more shameful to distrust our friends than to be deceived by them.

La Rochefoucauld

Build a little fence of
trust around today;
Fill the space with loving
work, and therein stay.

Frances Mary Buss

4

Old Friends

It has been said that the best mirror is an old friend. But a lifelong pal is more than a mirror; he or she is also a priceless treasure. Thomas Edison said, "I have friends whose friendship I would not swap for the favor of all the kings of the world." All of us know how Edison felt.

If you have an old friend you haven't called in a while, why not pick up the telephone today? The call won't cost much. And besides, the king has an unlisted number.

Ah, how good it feels!
　　　The hand of an old friend.
　　　　　　Henry Wadsworth Longfellow

Old friends are the great blessing of one's
later years. They have a memory of the same
events and have the same mode of thinking.
　　　　　　Horace Walpole

As in the case of wines that improve
with age, the oldest friendships ought to be
the most delightful.

　　　　　　Cicero

There is only one thing better than making a new friend, and that is keeping an old one.

Elmer G. Leterman

Real friendship is a slow grower.

Lord Chesterfield

The companions of our childhood always possess a certain power over our minds.

Mary Wollstonecraft Shelley

There is a magic in the memory of a schoolboy friendship. It softens the heart and even affects the nervous system of those who have no heart.

Benjamin Disraeli

There's no friend like someone who has known you since you were five.

Anne Stevenson

To be capable of steady friendship or lasting
love are the two greatest proofs, not only of
goodness of heart, but of strength of mind.

William Hazlitt

Happy is he to whom, in the maturer season
of life, there remains one tried
and constant friend.

Anna Letitia Barbauld

It is great to have friends when one is young,
but indeed it is still more so when you are
getting old. When we are young, friends are,
like everything else, a matter of course.
In the old days, we know what it means
to have them.

Edvard Grieg

Forsake not an old friend, for the new
is not comparable to him; a new friend
is as new wine.

The Bible, Ecclesiastes

A true friend is forever a friend.

George Macdonald

The best mirror is a trusted, old friend.

Sephardic Saying

An old friend never can be found,
and nature has provided that he cannot
easily be lost.

Samuel Johnson

Years and years of happiness only make us
realize how lucky we are to have friends
who have shared and made that happiness
a reality.

Robert E. Frederick

When you are young and without success,
you have only a few friends. Then, later on,
when you are rich and famous, you still have
a few... if you are lucky.

Pablo Picasso

It is one of the blessings of old friends that
you can afford to be stupid with them.

Ralph Waldo Emerson

I am learning to live close to the lives of my
friends without ever seeing them. No miles
can separate your soul from mine.

John Muir

Old friends are best
unless you catch a new
one fit to make an old one
out of.

Sarah Orne Jewett

5

A Helping Hand

The philosopher Seneca wrote, "Wherever there is a human being, there is an opportunity for kindness." We, like Seneca, are faced with countless opportunities to lend a helping hand. The following quotations should help you help.

Man absolutely cannot live by himself.

Erich Fromm

Everyone needs help from everyone.

Bertolt Brecht

No person was ever honored for what he
received. Honor has been the reward
for what he gave.

Calvin Coolidge

What is serving God? 'Tis doing good to man.

Poor Richard's Almanac

What we freely give,
forever is our own.

Granville

When you cease to make a contribution,
you begin to die.

Eleanor Roosevelt

Goodwill to others helps build you up.
It is good for your body. It is the real elixir
of life.

Prentice Mulford

The smallest actual good is better than the
most magnificent promise of impossibilities.

Macaulay

Even if it's a little thing, do something
for those who have need of help, something
for which you get no pay but the privilege
of doing it.

Albert Schweitzer

We cannot hold a torch to light another's
path without brightening our own.

Ben Sweetland

Give what you have. To someone else
it may be better than you dare to think.

Henry Wadsworth Longfellow

Find out how much God has given you and
from it take what you need; the remainder
is needed by others.

Saint Augustine

Live and let live is not enough;
live and help live is not too much.

Orison Swett Marden

When a person is down in the world,
an ounce of help is better than
a pound of preaching.

Edward Bulwer-Lytton

An ounce of help is worth a pound of pity.

Old Saying

Time and money spent in helping men
to do more for themselves is far better than
mere giving.

Henry Ford

The truest help we can render an afflicted
man is not to take his burden from him,
but to call out his best energy, that he
may be able to bear the burden.

Phillips Brooks

The greatest good you can do for another is not just to share your riches, but to reveal to him his own.

Benjamin Disraeli

We cannot live only for ourselves.
A thousand fibers connect us
with our fellow men.

Herman Melville

The service we render others is the rent
we pay for our room on earth.

Sir Wilfred Grenfell

To give pleasure to a single heart
by a single kind act is better than a thousand
head-bowings in prayer.

Saadi

I wonder why it is that we are not all kinder
to each other. How much the world needs it!
How easily it is done!

Henry Drummond

All altruism springs from putting yourself
in the other person's place.

Harry Emerson Fosdick

In the time we have, it is surely our duty
to do all the good we can to all the people
we can in all the ways we can.

William Barclay

I expect to pass through life but once.
If, therefore, there be any kindness I can
show, or any good thing I can do for any
fellow being, let me do it now,
as I shall not pass this way again.

William Penn

Help your brother's boat across,
and your own will reach the shore.

Hindu Proverb

It takes wisdom and discernment to minister
to people in need. We must look beyond
the apparent and seek to meet the needs
of the whole person.

Richard C. Chewning

The only gift is a portion of thyself.

Ralph Waldo Emerson

I hate the giving of the hand unless the
whole man accompanies it.

Ralph Waldo Emerson

Better to expose ourselves to ingratitude
than fail in assisting the unfortunate.

Du Coeur

We are cold to others only when we are dull
in ourselves.

William Hazlitt

The race of mankind would perish
did they cease to aid each other.

Sir Walter Scott

We secure our friends not by accepting favors
but by doing them.

Thucydides

Make yourself necessary to somebody.

Ralph Waldo Emerson

To pull a friend out
of the mire, don't hesitate
to get dirty.

Ba'al Shem Tov

6

The Joy of Giving

Any way you slice it, generosity is the icing on the cake of friendship. We human beings invest untold energy in the ancient and respected art of giving, and we do so for a very good reason: A thoughtful gift always enriches the giver as well as the recipient.

The Renaissance philosopher Erasmus wrote, "He does himself good who does good to his friend." Do yourself a favor and do one for a friend. Big-hearted giving is the surest way to have your cake and eat it too.

Every charitable act is a stepping-stone
toward heaven.

Henry Ward Beecher

We make a living by what we get,
but we make a life by what we give.

Norman MacEwan

Without kindness, there can be no true joy.

Thomas Carlyle

There is no happiness in having or in getting,
but only in giving.

Henry Drummond

An act of goodness is of itself an act of happiness.

Maurice Maeterlinck

So long as you can
sweeten another's pain,
life is not in vain.

Helen Keller

In about the same degree
as you are helpful,
you will be happy.

Karl Reiland

It is enough that I am of value to somebody
today.

Hugh Prather

When you learn to live for others,
they will live for you.

Paramahansa Yogananda

Happiness consists in giving
and in serving others.

Henry Drummond

 A n unshared life is not living.
He who shares does not lessen, but greatens,
his life.

Stephen S. Wise

 H e who does not live in some degree
for others, hardly lives for himself.

Michel de Montaigne

 A man wrapped up in himself makes
a very small bundle.

Benjamin Franklin

It is more blessed to give than to receive.

Acts 20:35

Provision for others is a fundamental
responsibility of human life.

Woodrow Wilson

God loveth a cheerful giver.

II Corinthians 9:7

7

The Pleasures of Friendship

The French essayist and aviator Antoine de Saint-Exupéry wrote, "There is no hope or joy except in human relations." Anyone who has experienced friendship in full bloom knows this statement to be true. Our friends and loved ones provide some of life's greatest delights, but the pleasures of friendship are never delivered on a one-way street. In order to gain happiness, we must first give it away.

Lord Chesterfield observed, "Pleasure is reciprocal; no one feels it who does not at the same time give it. To be pleased, one must please." In this chapter, we examine the two-way pleasures of friendship.

Friendship is the source of the greatest
pleasures, and without friends even the most
agreeable pursuits become tedious.

Saint Thomas Aquinas

A sympathetic friend can be quite as dear
as a brother.

Homer

To devote a portion of one's leisure to doing
something for someone else is one of the
highest forms of recreation.

Gerald B. Fitzgerald

Friendship ought to be a gratuitous joy,
like the joys afforded by art.

Simone Weil

The infectiously joyous
men and women are those
who forget themselves
in thinking about others
and serving others.

Robert J. McCracken

The real friend is he
or she who can share
all our sorrow and
double our joys.

B. C. Forbes

Arise, and eat bread, and let thine heart
be merry.

I Kings 21:7

One cannot have too large a party.
A large party secures its own amusement.

Jane Austen

The company makes the feast.

Old Saying

Happiness to me is enjoying my friends
and family.

Reba McEntire

Shared joys make a friend.

Friedrich Nietzsche

You meet your friend, your face brightens —
you have struck gold.

Kassia

I have learned that to have a good friend
is the purest of all God's gifts, for it is a love
that has no exchange of payment.

Frances Farmer

To get the full value of a joy you must have
somebody to divide it with.

Mark Twain

I feel the need of friendly discourse. I cannot miss this without feeling, as does any other intelligent man, a void and a deep need.

Vincent van Gogh

True happiness arises from the enjoyment of one's self and from the friendship and conversation of a few select companions.

Joseph Addison

A single conversation across the table with a wise man is worth a month's study of books.

Chinese Proverb

Good company and good discourse
are the very sinews of virtue.

Izaak Walton

Cheerful company shortens the miles.

German Proverb

It's not good to be alone — even in Paradise.

Old Saying

True happiness consists not in the multitude
of friends, but in the worth and choice.

Ben Jonson

8

Laughing with Friends

Few sounds on earth can compare with the reverberations of friends laughing together. Hearty laughter is oil in the engine of friendship: With laughter, things run smoothly; without it, the gears have a tendency to grind.

Arnold Glasow observed, "A loyal friend laughs at your jokes when they're not so good and sympathizes with your problems when they're not so bad." Herein, we consider the joys of a good laugh and the blessings of a good friend to share it with.

The clearest sign of wisdom is continued cheerfulness.

Michel de Montaigne

A cheerful friend is like a sunny day, which sheds its brightness on all around.

John Lubbock

There is no man that imparteth his joys
  to his friends, but he joyeth the more.

Francis Bacon

Nobody who is afraid of laughing,
  and heartily too, at his friend can be said
  to have a true and thorough love for him.

Julius Charles Hare

You grow up the day you have
    your first real laugh at yourself.

Ethel Barrymore

Learning to laugh at ourselves,
  we did not lack for things to laugh about.

Michael Ramsey, Archbishop of Canterbury

Laughter moves your internal organs around.
It is an igniter of great expectations.

Norman Cousins

Laughter need not be cut out of anything,
since it improves everything.

James Thurber

For me, a hearty "belly laugh" is one
of the most beautiful sounds in the world.

Bennett Cerf

Laugh, and the world laughs with you.

Ella Wheeler Wilcox

"Live to love" was my father's motto.
  "Live to laugh" is mine.

Hannah Cowley

The key to my locked spirit
      is your laughing mouth.

Nur Jahan

Laughter can be more satisfying than honor;
      more precious than money;
      more heart-cleansing than prayer.

Harriet Rochlin

God hath made me to laugh,
      so that all that hear will laugh with me.

Genesis 21:6

When good cheer is lacking, our friends will be packing.

Unknown

A good laugh is sunshine in a house.
William Makepeace Thackeray

The most thoroughly wasted of all days
is that on which one has not laughed.
Chamfort

The young man who has not wept is a savage,
and the old man who will not laugh is a fool.
George Santayana

Among those whom I like or admire,
I can find no common denominator,
but among those whom I love, I can:
All of them make me laugh.
W. H. Auden

The first day I gave a laugh, my tears were blown out like candles. It takes effort to push back the stone from the mouth of the tomb.

Mary Lavin

All who would win joy must share it; happiness was born a twin.

Lord Byron

Unshared joy is an unlit candle.

Spanish Proverb

Happiness is itself a kind of gratitude.

Joseph Wood Krutch

A man isn't poor if he can still laugh.

Raymond Hitchcock

The time to be happy is now. The way
to be happy is to make others so.

Robert Ingersoll

The best way to cheer yourself up
is to cheer up somebody else.

Mark Twain

Happiness is not perfected until it is shared.

Jane Porter

Wear a smile and have
friends; wear a scowl
and have wrinkles.

George Eliot

.

9

Friendship in Tough Times

Plato advised, "Be kind, for everyone you meet is fighting a hard battle." He might have added that sometimes the battle rages so fiercely that we must call in the reserves. Trusted friends are the reserve troops who help us survive and conquer the inevitable skirmishes of life.

Ovid observed, "As the yellow gold is tried in fire, so the faith of friendship must be seen in adversity." If you have an acquaintance who is being tested by fire, volunteer your services today. Who knows? Your support might just turn the tide of battle.

In prosperity our friends know us;
in adversity we know our friends.

John Churton Collins

The shifts of fortune test the reliability
of friends.

Cicero

Friendship makes prosperity more brilliant
and lightens adversity by dividing
and sharing it.

Cicero

Trouble shared is trouble halved.

Dorothy Sayers

No man can be happy without a friend
nor be sure of his friend till he is unhappy.

Thomas Fuller

The firmest friendships have been formed
in mutual adversity, as iron is most strongly
united by the fiercest flame.

Charles Caleb Colton

It is not so much our friends' help
that helps us, as the confidence of their help.

Epicurus

Oh Dear! How unfortunate I am not to have
anyone to weep with!

Madame de Sévigné

Real friendship is shown in times of trouble;
prosperity is full of friends.

Euripides

Prosperity makes friends;
adversity tries them.

Publilius Syrus

Prosperity is not a just scale; adversity is
the only balance to weigh friends.

Plutarch

The shifts of fortune test the reliability
of friends.

Cicero

Trouble is a sieve
through which we sift
our acquaintances. Those
too big to pass through
are our friends.

Arlene Francis

A friend in need is a friend indeed.

Old Saying

A friend should bear his friend's infirmities.

William Shakespeare

Sad things aren't the same
as depressing things.

Thornton Wilder

There are times when God asks nothing of his children except silence, patience and tears.

C. S. Robinson

There is no greater loan
than a sympathetic ear.

Frank Tyger

Friendship, of itself a holy tie,
   is made more sacred by adversity.

John Dryden

It's the friends you can call up at 4:00 a.m.
         that matter.

Marlene Dietrich

No matter what happens to you,
   if you can draw strength from God and the
people you love, nothing can ever defeat you.

Reba McEntire

In poverty and other misfortunes of life,
true friends are a sure refuge.

Aristotle

But every road is tough to me
that has no friend to cheer it.

Elizabeth Shane

The friend of my adversity I shall always
cherish most. I can better trust those who
helped to relieve the gloom of my dark hours
than those who are so ready to enjoy with me
the sunshine of my prosperity.

Ulysses S. Grant

Do not protect yourself by a fence
but rather by your friends.

Czechoslovakian Proverb

My friends have made
the story of my life.
In a thousand ways
they have turned my
limitations into beautiful
privileges and enabled me
to walk serene and happy
in the shadow
cast by my deprivation.

Helen Keller

To accept a favor from a friend
is to confer one.

John Churton Collins

The hearts that never lean must fall.

Emily Dickinson

The meek become known in anger,
the hero in war, and a friend in time of need.

Ibn Gabirol

The true way to soften one's troubles
is to solace those of others.

Madame de Maintenon

A cheer for the noble breast
That fears not danger's post;
And like the lifeboat, proves a friend,
When friends are wanted most.

Eliza Cook

When a friend is in trouble, don't annoy him by asking if there is anything you can do. Think up something appropriate and do it.

Edgar Watson Howe

10

All-Purpose Advice

Edna St. Vincent Millay wrote to a friend requesting, "Please give me some good advice in your next letter. I promise not to take it." On the following pages, we offer a potpourri of wisdom worth taking, no matter what your friends say.

If the world is cold, make it your business to build fires.

Horace Traubel

The best time to make friends is before you need them.

Ethel Barrymore

Friendship was given by nature to be an assistant to virtue, not a companion in vice.

Cicero

He that walketh with wise men shall be wise.

Solomon

Friendship with the upright is profitable.

Confucius

Do not remove a fly from your friend's forehead with a hatchet.

Chinese Proverb

Live so that your friends
can defend you,
but never have to.

Arnold Glasow

 Be courteous to all
but intimate with few,
and let those few be well
tried before you give
them your confidence.

George Washington

Be slow to fall into
friendship; but when
thou art in, continue firm
and constant.

Socrates

Fortify yourself with a flock of friends!
You can select them at random, write to one,
dine with one, visit one, or take your
problems to one. There is always at least
one who will understand, inspire, and give
you the lift you may need at the time.

George Matthew Adams

If two friends ask you to judge a dispute,
don't accept, because you will lose one
friend; on the other hand, if two strangers
come with the same request, accept,
because you will gain one friend.

Saint Augustine

Friendship is seldom lasting but between equals, or where the superiority on one side is reduced by some equivalent advantage on the other.

Samuel Johnson

Have no friends not equal to yourself.

Confucius

It is wise to pour the oil
of refined politeness
on the mechanism
of friendship.

Colette

A word of kindness is seldom spoken in vain, while witty sayings are as easily lost as the pearls slipping from a broken string.

George Prentice

Seek those who find your road agreeable, your personality and mind stimulating, your philosophy acceptable, and your experiences helpful. Let those who do not seek their own kind.

Henri Fabre

Never claim as a right what you can ask as a favor.

John Churton Collins

Since there is nothing so well worth having as friends, never lose a chance to make them.

Francesco Guicciardini

The secret of being tiresome is to tell everything.

Voltaire

Silence is a friend who will never betray.

Confucius

Men only become friends by community
of pleasures.

Samuel Johnson

Friendship that flames goes out in a flash.

Thomas Fuller

It is the peculiar quality of a fool to perceive
the faults of others and to forget his own.

Cicero

Hate the sin and love the sinner.

Mahandas Gandhi

Often we can help each other most by
leaving each other alone; at other times we
need the handgrasp and the word of cheer.

Elbert Hubbard

When someone does something good,
applaud! You'll make two people happy.

Samuel Goldwyn

Nothing is ever lost by courtesy.
It is the cheapest of pleasures, costs nothing,
and conveys much. It pleases him who gives
and receives and thus, like mercy,
is twice blessed.

Erastus Wiman

Advice is what we ask for when we already
know the answer but wish we didn't.

Erica Jong

The true secret of giving advice is to be
perfectly indifferent whether it is taken
or not.

Hannah Whitall Smith

Never explain — your friends do not need it,
and your enemies will not believe you
anyway.

Elbert Hubbard

The man who thinks he can live without
others is mistaken; the one who thinks others
can't live without him is even more deluded.

Hasidic Saying

Tell me thy company, and I'll tell thee
what thou art.

Miguel de Cervantes

The wise man seeks a friend with qualities
which he himself lacks.

Jeremy Taylor

Associate yourself with men of good quality
if you esteem your own reputation, for 'tis
better to be alone than in bad company.

George Washington

"Stay" is a charming word
in a friend's vocabulary.

Louisa May Alcott

The most called-upon prerequisite of a friend is an accessible ear.

Maya Angelou

To be pleased, one must please.

Lord Chesterfield

11

Observations

We conclude with a potpourri of worldly
wisdom about fabulous friendships. Enjoy!

Friendship begins with gratitude.

George Eliot

Friendship is the only
cement that will ever hold
the world together.

Woodrow Wilson

Wherever you are, it is your friends
who make your world.

William James

Robbing life of friendship is like robbing
the world of the sun.

Cicero

Life is partly what we make it and partly
what is made by the friends we choose.

Chinese Proverb

There is no wilderness like a life
without friends.

Baltasar Gracián

Friendship is not quick to burn.

May Sarton

I have three chairs in my house;
    one for solitude, two for friendship,
      and three for society.

Henry David Thoreau

There are three types of friends: some are
like food — indispensable; some are like
medicine — good occasionally; and some
are like poison — to be avoided always.

Ibn Gabirol

Constant use will not wear ragged the fabric
of friendship.

Dorothy Parker

Friends — real friends — reserve nothing.

Euripides

We have no more right to put our discordant states of mind into the lives of those around us and rob them of their sunshine and brightness than we have to enter their houses and steal their silverware.

Julia Seton

There are only two people who can tell you the truth about yourself — an enemy who has lost his temper and a friend who loves you dearly.

Antisthenes

Good friends, good books and a sleepy conscience: This is the ideal life.

Mark Twain

Friendship has splendors that love knows not.

Mariama Bâ

Friends aren't any
more important than
breath or blood to
a high school senior.

Betty Ford

That friendship will not continue to the end
which is begun for an end.

Francis Quarles

The reward of friendship is itself.
The man who hopes for anything else does
not understand what true friendship is.

Saint Alfred of Rievaulx

Friendship is always a sweet responsibility,
never an opportunity.

Kahlil Gibran

The worst solitude is to be destitute of sincere friendship.

Francis Bacon

Friendship is almost always the union
of a part of one mind with a part of another.

George Santayana

Perhaps the most delightful friendships
are those in which there is much agreement,
much disputation, and yet more
personal liking.

George Eliot

Animals are such agreeable friends — they
ask no questions, they pass no criticisms.

George Eliot

Without wearing any mask
that we are conscious of,
we have a special face
for each friend.

Oliver Wendell Holmes, Sr.

Friendships, like geraniums, bloom in kitchens.

Blanche H. Gelfant

We cannot tell the precise moment when friendship is formed. As in filling a vessel drop by drop, there is at last a drop which makes it run over. So in a series of kindnesses there is, at last, one which makes the heart run over.

James Boswell

Every organism requires an environment of friends, partly to shield it from violent changes, and partly to supply it with its wants.

Alfred North Whitehead

A good laugh is good for the spirits, it's true; but a good cry is good for the soul.

Bette Midler

Think where man's glory most begins and ends, And say my glory was I had such friends.

W. B. Yeats

A man cannot be said
to succeed in this life
who does not satisfy
one friend.

Henry David Thoreau

To associate with other like-minded people
in small purposeful groups is for the great
majority of men and women a source
of profound psychological satisfaction.

Aldous Huxley

No one person can possibly combine
all the elements supposed to make up what
everyone means by friendship.

Francis Marion Crawford

If you want an accounting of your worth,
count your friends.

Merry Browne

Gossip is nature's telephone.

Sholem Aleichem

Duty towards God is to be happy;
   duty towards a neighbor is to give him
      pleasure and alleviate his pain.

W. H. Auden

To be capable of steady friendship or lasting
love are the two greatest proofs, not only of
goodness of heart, but of strength of mind.

William Hazlitt

We have really no absent friends.

Elizabeth Bowen

Friends are the family
we choose for ourselves.

Edna Buchanan

One thing everybody in the world wants and needs is friendliness.

William E. Holler

The really serious things in life are earning one's living and loving one's neighbor.

W. H. Auden

Age doesn't protect you from love. But love, to some extent, protects you from age.

Jeanne Moreau

The great tragedy of life is not that men perish but that they cease to love.

Somerset Maugham

Nobody, but nobody, can make it out here alone.

Maya Angelou

Funny, you don't look like a friend. Ah, but they never do.

Grace Metalious

Sources

Sources

Sources

Edna St. Vincent Millay 113
Mary Russell Mitford 24
Michel de Montaigne 79, 90
Jeanne Moreau 151
Toni Morrison 23
John Muir 59
Prentice Mulford 64
Charles B. Newcomb 51
Friedrich Nietzsche 86
Anaïs Nin 22, 35
Kathleen Norris 26
Ovid 101
Dorothy Parker 137
Blaise Pascal 33
William Penn 43, 69
Pablo Picasso 59
Marge Piercy 31
Plato 101
Plutarch 104
Mary Pettibone Poole 39
Jane Porter 99
Hugh Prather 78
George Prentice 123
Publilius Syrus 48, 104
Francis Quarles 141
Michael Ramsey 92
Karl Reiland 77
Agnes Repplier 30
Cardinal de Retz 46
C. S. Robinson 106
La Rochefoucauld 51
Harriet Rochlin 94
Eleanor Roosevelt 28, 64
Margaret Lee Runbeck 42
Dagobert D. Runes 27
Saadï 68
Antoine de Saint-Exupéry 81
George Santayana 96, 143
May Sarton 137
Dorothy Sayers 102

Charles M. Schwab 43
Albert Schweitzer 64
Walter Scott 71
Seneca 38, 50, 61
Julia Seton 138
Madame de Sévigné 103
William Shakespeare 50, 106
Elizabeth Shane 109
Mary Wollstonecraft Shelley 56
Fulton J. Sheen 43
Hannah Whitall Smith 128
Socrates 119
Solomon 116
Sophocles 21, 36
Anne Stevenson 56
Robert Louis Stevenson 17
Henry Stimson 47
Ben Sweetland 65
Jeremy Taylor 129
William Makepeace Thackeray 96
Saint Thomas Aquinas 82
Henry David Thoreau 137, 147
Thucydides 71
James Thurber 93
Horace Traubel 114
Mark Twain 86, 98, 138
Frank Tyger 107
George M. Verity 37
Voltaire 124
Horace Walpole 54
Izaak Walton 88
William Arthur Ward 35
Mercy Otis Warren 22
George Washington 36, 118, 129
Simone Weil 82
Frances Ward Weller 23
Rebecca West 31
Betty White 33
Alfred North Whitehead 146
Ella Wheeler Wilcox 93